Everyday
GRATITUDE

Spiritual Refreshment
for Women

REBECCA CURRINGTON

BARBOUR
PUBLISHING

© 2013 Barbour Publishing, Inc.

Writing and compilation by Rebecca Currington in association with Snapdragon Group℠ Editorial Services.

Print ISBN 978-1-63609-042-9

Adobe Digital Edition (.epub) 978-1-63609-227-0

Published by Barbour Publishing, Inc., 1810 Barbour Drive, Uhrichsville, Ohio 44683
www.barbourbooks.com

Our mission is to inspire the world with the life-changing message of the Bible.

Printed in the United States of America.

Contents

Enter into [God's]
gates with thanksgiving,
and into his courts with praise:
be thankful unto him,
and bless his name.

PSALM 100:4 KJV

Introduction

*I will praise God in a song and
will honor him by giving thanks.*
PSALM 69:30 NCV

. . . .

Around the world, people worship many gods. Some worship gods of wood and stone. Some worship fire or water, some success, and others worship money and possessions. How sad it is that these objects of worship cannot breathe or speak or hear prayers; they aren't able to help when trouble looms and threatens to overwhelm. But we worship a living God, the Creator of all things. Though just and holy, our God is also loving and tenderhearted. He breathes and speaks and hears. Of all the people on planet earth, those who worship the name of

the Lord should be thankful, for He is alive! He cares when we are hurting; He has the power and the willingness to help us in our time of need.

No book on earth could contain all of God's goodness. But these humble pages are dedicated to thankfulness, for all things great and small, in the highs of life as well as in the valleys. In life's momentous moments and the ordinary moments we live each and every day. We hope your heart will swell with thankfulness and joy as you read these pages, for our God is a great God. He is good and generous and kind. As you read, be sure to keep a pen and paper nearby to record your personal thoughts of thanks.

Acceptance

MORE THAN A NUMBER

*"Man looks at the outward appearance,
but the LORD looks at the heart."*
1 SAMUEL 16:7 NKJV

. . . .

No one likes to be reduced to a number. But in our world, that's exactly what happens. We each have a social security number, a phone number, a driver's license number, a bank account number, and on and on. But God doesn't see any one of us as a number. The Bible says He calls us by name. He sees our hearts, not just our photo IDs. And because He loves us all personally, we should thank Him personally too.

HIS BELOVED

He made us accepted in the Beloved.
Ephesians 1:6 NKJV

. . . .

God loves and accepts us. His only desire is that we grow to become the people He created us to be. We can rest in that. But God has done more. He also knows that we need the acceptance of others. True, we will never have acceptance with everyone. But there is one group we fit into—those who love God, His beloved. Give thanks to our heavenly Father, for He has made us part of His family.

Accountability

THE NINE

Jesus asked, "Didn't I heal ten men?
Where are the other nine?"
LUKE 17:17 NLT

In the New Testament we read that ten lepers came to Jesus one morning asking to be healed. Jesus healed all ten of them—but only one came back to thank Him. Jesus looked around and asked where the other nine had gone. We should always remember to thank God for all the times He has rescued us, for all the gifts He has given us, for all the love and compassion and forgiveness He has bestowed on us.

A NOTE OF THANKS

*I will sacrifice a thank offering to you
and call on the name of the LORD.*
PSALM 116:17

. . . .

When we receive a gift, it's proper etiquette to write a note of thanks. This formality serves a dual purpose. Not only does the note of thanks bless the giver of the gift, but it also helps the receiver to acknowledge the gift and appreciate its value. We may tell ourselves that God knows we are grateful, but in order to fully enjoy His blessings, we should offer our words of thanks.

Adversity

THANKS FOR MY TROUBLE

*Our light and momentary troubles
are achieving for us an eternal glory
that far outweighs them all.*
2 CORINTHIANS 4:17

· ·

We've all said "thanks for your trouble" when someone goes out of their way to help us out. But how often do we say "thanks for my trouble"? And yet, it is often in times of adversity that so many good things happen to us. We grow in depth of character. We gain compassion for others. And we have an opportunity to move closer to God and experience His loving care. Adversity brings much to be thankful for.

WHY ADVERSITY?

[Jesus answered], "In this world you
will have trouble. But take heart!
I have overcome the world."
JOHN 16:33

. . . .

We have all asked why there has to be adversity
in the world. Only God knows the whole answer,
but we can be sure of this: adversity is to the soul
what exercise is to the body. As we struggle against
our circumstances and place complete trust in
our heavenly Father, we are working our spiritual
muscles, growing in strength and confidence. We
can thank God even for the hard times.

Affliction

TEMPORARY HOUSES

Be joyful in hope, patient in affliction,
faithful in prayer.
ROMANS 12:12

• •

The Bible teaches that our bodies are little more than temporary houses for our souls. But when our bodies are hurting, they sure seem like much more. God acknowledges and understands our physical pain. After all, His Son, Jesus, experienced extraordinary suffering in His physical body. When you're hurting, look to Jesus, reach out to Him. He will be there to comfort and sustain you.

A HEALING BALM

Many are the afflictions of the righteous,
but the LORD delivers him out of them all.
PSALM 34:19 NKJV

. . . .

We will all experience affliction of some kind at one
time or another in this world. It is part of the human
condition. But when we put our trust in God, we
can know for certain that any—and all—afflictions
are temporary. Even if they follow us throughout our
lives, God has prepared for each of us a new body
free from pain and suffering. One day we will be
with Him, and we will never hurt again. Praise God!

Angels

THE MINISTRY OF ANGELS

Are not all angels spirits in the divine service,
sent to serve for the sake of those
who are to inherit salvation?
HEBREWS 1:14 NRSV

- -

Almost all children believe in angels, but it seems that when we get older, most of us relegate heavenly beings to imagination and folklore. The thing is, it just isn't so. The Bible is filled with angelic encounters and interventions. We are told that angels serve God, in part, by looking after us. How precious we must be to our heavenly Father, and how grateful we should be that He would direct the angels on our behalf.

VOICES OF ANGELS

Bless the LORD, O you his angels,
you mighty ones who do his bidding,
obedient to his spoken word.
PSALM 103:20 NRSV

The Bible tells us that even the mighty angels of God, His messengers in the heavens, are blessing the Lord and are thankful to Him. Imagine how that must sound, all those powerful angelic voices lifting their praises to Him. How can we humans do less? We, who have been created in God's own image, who have been given free will? Of all God's creatures, we are most blessed!

Belief

BELIEVE OR DENY

*Anyone who comes to God must believe
that he is real and that he rewards
those who truly want to find him.*
HEBREWS 11:6 NCV

. . . .

Some people actually believe that the beauty and
diversity that surround us are the result of nothing
more than lucky chance, happy accidents. But then
again, humans have a long history of believing the
absurd. At one point, scientists and astronomers
even concluded that the earth was not only flat, but
also the center of the universe. We can be thankful
that our God has not hidden Himself from us—He
has shown Himself. To deny the obvious would be
nothing short of ridiculous.

GOD'S IMPOSSIBILITIES

*Jesus said to him, "If you can believe,
all things are possible to him who believes."*
MARK 9:23 NKJV

. . . .

Is anything impossible for God? The natural response would be no, but not so fast! He can't take us into the realm of the impossible unless we believe. He doesn't ask us to believe in the impossibility itself, but rather in His power and greatness, in His ability to do what is needed as well as His willingness to act on our behalf. All things are possible for us simply because all things are possible for Him.

Blessings

ONE BY ONE

*All these blessings shall come upon you
and overtake you, because you obey
the voice of the LORD your God.*
DEUTERONOMY 28:2 NKJV

. . . .

An old, familiar song urges us, "Count your blessings, name them one by one." Naming each specific blessing poses a real challenge because there are so many of them. Our God is more generous than we could ever imagine. He is always looking for ways to make us smile. Even on the most challenging, painful days, there are still brilliant sunsets and flowering trees, the laughter of children, and the hope of tomorrow. We all have reason to count our blessings!

BLESSING GOD

Bless the LORD, O my soul;
And all that is within me,
bless His holy name!
PSALM 103:1 NKJV

. . . .

We all know that God pours out His blessings on us, but we may not fully understand that we can bless Him in return. We bless Him when we obey His commandments, which were given to keep us safe from harm and heartache. We bless Him when we forgive others as He has forgiven us. And we bless Him when we come before Him with hearts bursting with thankfulness for all He has done.

Change

CHANGE IS GOOD

Be made new in the attitude of your minds.
EPHESIANS 4:23

. . . .

Some people embrace change, but most of us don't. We prefer to settle in and get comfortable. A lack of change, though, never produces good results. It leads to stagnation and decay. Without change, there is no life, no movement. God knows it's difficult for us to accept change, but He asks us to be grateful for it and to trust Him in it. He promises to always be there with us when change comes our way.

OUR ROCK

*Jesus Christ is the same yesterday
and today and forever.*
HEBREWS 13:8 NASB

. . . .

Change is often good for us. We need to move and
grow and become who God created us to be. But
it's different for God. He doesn't change. He doesn't
need to. He is already all and all and all—He is
complete. We can be grateful that when the world
is spinning, the heavenly Father is our anchor, our
rock. What He says today holds true for tomorrow
and the next day and the day after that. He will
always love us.

Circumstances

STORM CLOUDS

Rejoice always, pray continually,
give thanks in all circumstances,
for this is God's will for you in Christ Jesus.
1 THESSALONIANS 5:16–18

. . . .

It's easy to give thanks when things are going well and not so easy when storm clouds are hovering overhead. But there is one thing we can give thanks for in every circumstance of our lives: we will never walk through a storm alone. God is with us. He has promised never to leave us nor forsake us. His love and comfort and strength are always available. All we need to do is ask.

IT'S ALL RELATIVE

*I have learned to be content
whatever the circumstances.*
PHILIPPIANS 4:11

. . . .

We look around and see how others live. Then we say to ourselves, "If I had a sweet deal like that, I'd never ask for anything else." It doesn't matter, though, if our idea of a sweet deal is a great relationship, lots of money, fame, or some other circumstance that we think would make our lives amazing. We all have challenges and pain. No exceptions. But we can thank God that He is there for us regardless of our circumstances.

Comfort

OUR TEARS

This is what the LORD says: . . .
"I will comfort you as a mother
comforts her child."
ISAIAH 66:12–13 NCV

. . . .

Grief, sorrow, and mourning are all part of the human experience. No one escapes—not the rich, the poor, the old, the young. . . We call it "the downside" of life. It is in those moments, however, those painful times of intense sadness and suffering that God has promised His comfort. And He also promises that one day He will banish all sorrow and crying from the face of the earth. Thank God for His promises.

WHAT WE DON'T DESERVE

The LORD wants to show his mercy to you.
He wants to rise and comfort you.
ISAIAH 30:18 NCV

. . . .

No one enjoys sadness and sorrow, and yet we often bring it on ourselves. We make poor choices, dismissing the wisdom of others and even the discernment God places in our hearts. But when it all falls apart and we come to our senses, we find in God what we don't deserve. Like a loving father, He reaches out to us and comforts our aching hearts. His great love and mercy surround us.

Commandments

HAPPY AND FREE

*If you obey all the decrees and commands
I am giving you today, all will be well
with you and your children.*
DEUTERONOMY 4:40 NLT

. . . .

We love our children. We want them to be happy and free. Still we saddle them with, shall we say, our commandments: "Stay out of the street," we tell them. "Don't play with matches." The list is long. Our intention is not to spoil their fun but to keep them safe from dangers they often can't even imagine. Remember, God's commandments are backed by the same purpose—to assure our safety and well-being.

ALL ABOUT LOVE

Praise the LORD! Blessed is the man who fears the LORD, who delights greatly in His commandments.
PSALM 112:1 NKJV

. . . .

Not only are God's commandments intended to keep us safe and well, they are also designed to help us reach our maximum potential. The superficial things we might be asked to give up to honor Him can never compare to the rewards that obeying His instructions are certain to bring. God is a wise and loving Father who wants to see us become all we can be. His commandments are intended to help us get there.

Confidence

WHAT'S BEST

"Blessed is the one who trusts in the LORD,
whose confidence is in him."

JEREMIAH 17:7

. . . .

We place our confidence in all kinds of things these days—the stock market, our paychecks, the schools our children attend, the stores where we shop, our marriages. . . We do this knowing these things can and often do fail us. But when it comes to God, our confidence is always well placed. Though He may do things differently than we expect, He is always doing what is best.

FACING OUR TROUBLES

*Thus says the Lord GOD, . . . "In quietness
and confidence shall be your strength."*
ISAIAH 30:15 NKJV

· ·

When things go wrong in our lives, we often become
upset and agitated. This is a normal human response. Thankfully, God has given us an alternative.
He asks that we quiet our minds, refusing to give
in to the rush of troubling thoughts and images.
He then says to focus on Him—putting our complete
confidence in Him. Doing this lifts us out of the
waters that are churning around us and into God's
capable hands.

Conscience

ADVANCE WARNING

*Let us draw near to God with a sincere heart
and with the full assurance that faith brings,
having our hearts sprinkled to cleanse us
from a guilty conscience.*
HEBREWS 10:22

· ·

Many times we think of our conscience as a guilt
generator. But in reality, a conscience is one of the
most precious gifts God has given us. He meant it
to be an internal sensor, designed to let us know
when we're in danger of making an unwise choice
or engaging in questionable behavior that will
later result in painful consequences. How thankful
we should be to God for placing this advance
warning system inside each of us.

GENTLE REMINDER

The goal of this command is love,
which comes from a pure heart and
a good conscience and a sincere faith.
1 TIMOTHY 1:5

Not only do our consciences warn us about danger ahead, they also help us rightly evaluate our spiritual and emotional well-being. When our consciences are clear, we have confidence that we are on the path to becoming the women God intended us to be. When our consciences are stressed and gloomy, we are reminded that we must go to God and make things right. Without them, we might miss the joy of receiving God's grace and forgiveness.

Contentment

UNIQUE AND WONDERFUL

The fear of the LORD leads to life:
then one rests content.
PROVERBS 19:23

. . . .

It was once enough to be pretty, but now the search is for perfection in every physical feature. What so many women find out—often too late—is that physical perfection is not the path to happiness. It's better to thank God each day for the unique and wonderful way He has created each of us than to always be searching for some illusive appearance. God cares nothing for the world's idea of beauty. Let us be content, for we are His lovely masterpieces.

ONLY GOD CAN SATISFY

I say it is better to be content with what little you have. Otherwise, you will always be struggling for more, and that is like chasing the wind.
ECCLESIASTES 4:6 NCV

• •

How much is enough? No one seems to know. Millions of dollars once defined wealth, but now it's counted in billions. One nice car was once the standard, but now a whole garage full of cars is not enough. Our selfish human minds will always be grasping for more and more and more. We think more will bring us acceptance and security, but instead we should thank God alone who offers us lasting contentment.

Creation

CREATIVE WONDER

God saw all that he had made,
and it was very good.

GENESIS 1:31

. . . .

God's creative hand is everywhere—from creatures so small they are only visible through a microscope, to objects in space so large that their parameters are beyond our comprehension. Our understated appraisal is simply that they are all beautiful and unique. With each sunset, flowering tree, and ocean wave, our hearts fill with thankfulness and admiration. To think that such an Artist sees beauty in us is truly a wonder.

IN HIS IMAGE

*God said, "Let us make humankind in
our image, according to our likeness."*
GENESIS 1:26 NRSV

. . . .

When we look around us at the creative power and
genius of God, we should remember that we were
created in His image—which means His creative
bent exists within each of us. That bent may express
itself in the kitchen, the garden, or on the potter's
wheel. We may see it in clothing and jewelry design,
or strokes on a canvas. The ways in which creativity
can be expressed is endless. But in every case, we
can thank our heavenly Father for passing on the
joy of creating to His children.

Determination

KNOWING GOD

*Let us hold unswervingly to
the hope we profess.*
HEBREWS 10:23

· ·

Our determination to see something through
is directly linked to the value we place on that
something. For example, we are determined to
meet our educational goals because we can see a
better job and a bigger paycheck in our future. In
the same way, we can know what value we place on
our relationship with God by how often we express
our thanks and make room for Him in our lives.

FIRMLY RESOLVED

So let's not get tired of doing what is good.
At just the right time we will reap a harvest
of blessing if we don't give up.
GALATIANS 6:9 NLT

. . . .

The word determined means "to be firmly resolved and unwavering." It is the characteristic that keeps us from giving up and forfeiting the benefits of our good choices and hard work. God doesn't want us to miss out on any of His promises or the rewards He has prepared for us. We show Him our gratitude and trust when we cling tight to our faith, even when the outlook is less than promising. He has never given up on us—how could we do any less for Him?

Difficulties

ASKING FOR HELP

For Christ's sake, I delight in weaknesses,
in insults, in hardships, in persecutions,
in difficulties. For when I am weak,
then I am strong.

2 CORINTHIANS 12:10

. . . .

We all go through difficult times and tackle difficult projects. We make difficult decisions and learn difficult lessons. We deal with difficult people and seek answers for difficult questions. Often these things are more difficult than they really need to be—all because we fail to ask for God's help. Why would we ever face our difficulties alone when our heavenly Father has promised to be there when we call on Him?

WORKING OUT

*We are hard-pressed on every side, yet not
crushed; we are perplexed, but not in
despair; persecuted, but not forsaken;
struck down, but not destroyed.*

2 CORINTHIANS 4:8–9 NKJV

· ·

The difficulties in our lives are like a good workout
program. Hard situations toughen us up and give us
opportunities to strengthen our spiritual muscles.
We learn patience, faithfulness, perseverance, and
humility. We learn that God is worthy of our trust
and that He has given us full access to His wisdom
and guidance. We should look at life's hardships as
occasions to grow stronger in every area of our lives.

Doubt

DEALING WITH DOUBT

What if some were unfaithful?
Will their unfaithfulness nullify
God's faithfulness? Not at all!
ROMANS 3:3-4

· ·

It's time to demystify the word doubt. After all, it's just what we humans do. At one time or another, we doubt almost everything, including ourselves. And when it comes to God, He doesn't exist because we believe He does. He exists whether or not we believe He does. We haven't conjured Him up like Santa Claus or the Tooth Fairy. Thankfully, God isn't worried about our moments of doubt—and consequently, we shouldn't worry either.

NO DOUBT

The father instantly cried out, "I do believe,
but help me overcome my unbelief!"
MARK 9:24 NLT

. . . .

Truth is truth, and our moments of doubt cannot alter it in the least. But doubt can make it difficult for us to enter into relationship with God. We may doubt our worthiness to receive His blessings. We may doubt that we can be fully forgiven. We may doubt that God is able and willing to keep His promises. Those moments of doubt can cost us big time unless we ask God to help us overcome our doubt. Ask Him for His help today!

Discernment

IT'S ALL SPIN

Preserve sound judgment and discretion;
they will be life for you.
PROVERBS 3:21–22

. . . .

We live in a world where we can't trust our eyes and ears. Photographs and recordings can be altered. Everything is spin. . .smoke and mirrors. Never has there been a time when discernment was needed more. True discernment, defined as "keenness of insight," comes from God. It's that little voice inside your head that says, "Wait. . .something's not right here." Listen for it. Trust it. Thank God for it. It's there to help us navigate murky waters.

THROUGH THE WORDS

*I am your servant; give me discernment
that I may understand your statutes.*
PSALM 119:125

. . . .

The Bible is a big book with lots of nuances, sub-texts, cultural influences, and language barriers. But it is, first and foremost, the Word of God. What may be confusing and even overwhelming to the average mind is beautifully clear and simple when read with God's help. With the discernment from our heavenly Father, we are able to see the message, the context, and the truth flowing through the words. And we can thank Him for eyes to see.

Encouragement

ALWAYS NEEDED

If your gift is to encourage others,
be encouraging.
ROMANS 12:8 NLT

. . . .

Some people have a knack for gift-giving, but for most of us, it's tricky business. There is one gift, however, that is always welcome, always needed, and it costs us nothing in the way of dimes and dollars. We don't have to make a trip to the mall to find it either. That gift is encouragement—a simple message that lifts someone's weary mind and troubled heart. It's a gift that inspires thankfulness in both the giver and the receiver.

AN ENCOURAGING WORD

Everything that was written in the past was written to teach us, so that through the endurance taught in the Scriptures and the encouragement they provide we might have hope.

ROMANS 15:4

• •

This world we live in is not a friendly place for those of us who love God. Daily we face confusion and distractions. But, as we read God's Word and hear His name proclaimed, our hearts and minds are encouraged to keep going, keep believing the truth. We are better able to focus on the things of God. And we are better able to encourage and inspire hope in those around us.

Equality

THE GREAT EQUALIZER

*There is neither Jew nor Gentile, neither slave
nor free, nor is there male and female,
for you are all one in Christ Jesus.*
GALATIANS 3:28

· ·

We like to think we live in a world where everyone gets an equal shake. But that couldn't be further from the truth. Even in places where equality is valued, there are still people who have more money, better opportunities, and additional rights. Thankfully, God is the great equalizer. He sees each person who comes to Him as His own precious child. We all have equal access to Him. Equality is a reality only in the kingdom of God.

ALL THINGS EQUAL

*Christ Jesus: Who, being in very nature God,
did not consider equality with God something to
be used to his own advantage; rather, he made
himself nothing by taking the very nature of a
servant, being made in human likeness.*

PHILIPPIANS 2:5–7

When Jesus Christ, God's Son, the King of heaven, came to earth, He could have arranged to be born into a prominent or even royal family. But He wanted to level the playing field for all mankind, so He came into the lowest of human conditions, born in a crude structure used to house animals. In this way, He made us His equals and called us His sisters and brothers. Thanks be to God!

Eternal Life

STOP AND CONSIDER

*Keep yourselves in God's love as you wait
for the mercy of our Lord Jesus Christ
to bring you to eternal life.*
JUDE 1:21

• •

What would we do if we knew we had only a few more days to live? What would we do if we knew we had all of eternity to live? Either way, our lives would probably change drastically. Our priorities would be reordered, and we might even rethink the direction our lives are taking. None of us knows how many days we have left on this earth. But if we belong to God, all eternity has opened before us. We should live accordingly.

WHAT WE DESERVE

*God gives us the free gift of life
forever in Christ Jesus our Lord.*

ROMANS 6:23 NCV

. . . .

A TV ad claimed that everyone deserves a great smile. Of course, it was touting the services of a local dentist. But the truth is we don't deserve anything. And yet God has prepared so many wonderful things for us, like the amazing gift of eternal life. No, we don't deserve to be forgiven and adopted by a loving heavenly Father. We don't deserve to spend eternity with Him. But we can accept His gifts and thank Him for giving us so much more than we deserve.

Faith

RESTING IN FAITH

Some trust in chariots and some in horses,
but we trust in the name of the LORD our God.
PSALM 20:7

• •

There is no such thing as a person who has no faith. We all put our faith in something. . . the only question is what? For each of us, it's that thing we trust the most. Sometimes we put all our faith in ourselves and our ability to survive or succeed. But doesn't that sound like a difficult way to live? When we put our faith in God, we can rest in His power and wisdom and insight. No more struggling.

MOVING MOUNTAINS

*[Jesus] replied, "Truly I tell you, if you have
faith as small as a mustard seed, you can say
to this mountain, 'Move from here to there' and it
will move. Nothing will be impossible for you."*
MATTHEW 17:20

. . . .

Faith is a powerful thing. It can restore lives and bring
families together. It can heal the sick and provide
for our needs, even in extreme circumstances.
With the eyes of faith, we can see beyond our pain
and struggles. Yes, faith is powerful. Jesus told
His disciples that a tiny bit of faith—the size of a
mustard seed—could move a mountain. We can
thank God that even the tiniest faith is powerful
enough to conquer the biggest problem.

Faithfulness

TIME AFTER TIME

*Your steadfast love, O LORD, extends to the
heavens, your faithfulness to the clouds.*
PSALM 36:5 NRSV

. . . .

What does faithfulness mean? When we are faithful,
we show ourselves worthy of the faith others have
placed in us. When others are counting on us, we
come through, not just once, but time after time. God
is our example of faithfulness. He may not always
give us what we ask for or answer our prayers in
the way we expect, but He always comes through
for us, time after time after time.

COUNT ON IT

The Spirit produces the
fruit of. . .faithfulness.
GALATIANS 5:22 NCV

. . . .

When God resides within us, it shows. All kinds of
good things come flowing out of us, and one of those
good things is faithfulness. God is consistently,
unfailingly faithful. We always know we can count
on Him to keep His promises, treat us like His
precious children, forgive us when we confess our
sins, meet our needs when we are lacking. . . And
when God's Spirit dwells in us, we too, can walk in
faithfulness to Him and others.

Family

DEFINING FAMILY

A wise woman strengthens her family.
PROVERBS 14:1 NCV

. . . .

Family is a big word and difficult to define. Some
would say family consists exclusively of those who
are biologically connected. Others say it includes
all those we call our loved ones, regardless of the
blood bond. We call those who live by faith in God
"the family of God." However we define family, we
should cherish those God has placed in our lives.
They are among His greatest gifts.

ACTING LIKE FAMILY

*Behold, how good and how pleasant it is
for brethren to dwell together in unity!*
PSALM 133:1 KJV

God's family, like every other family, is made up of individuals with differing opinions and unique personalities. It takes love and understanding and forgiveness to make the family of God useful and effective in serving God, each other, and the world. But when this amazing dynamic comes together—members walking hand in hand—there is no more powerful force on earth. Thanks be to God for making us His sons and daughters united in His name.

Fellowship

GOD WELCOMES US

*Our fellowship is with the Father
and with his Son, Jesus Christ.*
1 JOHN 1:3

. . . .

It's difficult to imagine that almighty God would want to have fellowship with us. Next to Him, we are puny and insignificant. Yet, again and again, God's Word reminds us that He wants us to know Him, to spend time with Him, to be in a vital, loving relationship with Him. God has torn down the wall that separated us from Him and invited us into His presence. We may never completely understand why He loves us, but we can certainly enjoy His company.

SHARING FELLOWSHIP

If we live in the light, as God is in the light,
we can share fellowship with each other.
1 JOHN 1:7 NCV

. . . .

When we live in fellowship with God, everything
in and around us is transformed. That includes our
relationships with others. As we spend time in the
light of the heavenly Father's presence, we become
more loving, more caring, more forgiving. We grow
more patient and understanding. Differences and
resentments melt away. Fellowship with God opens
the way for us to have fellowship with others. We
can thank Him for reconciling us to Him—and to
each other.

Finances

IN ITS PLACE

Whoever loves wealth is never
satisfied with their income.
ECCLESIASTES 5:10

. . . .

Some people think it's spiritual to say they don't care about money. But here on this earth, we have to care. The important thing is that we keep money in its proper place in our lives. It cannot take center stage. We can't place our faith in money or expect money to rescue us in tough times. When we do, we put money in the place of God. Instead, we should always look to the heavenly Father for direction in how we use our money. He will never lead us in the wrong direction.

EVERY STEP

Turn my heart toward your statutes
and not toward selfish gain.
PSALM 119:36

Money is like a mirror for our souls. If there is greed in our hearts—or any jealousy, selfishness, laziness, or other dark desire—money will bring it to the surface. Money also has the ability to expose positive characteristics—like kindness, generosity, and honesty. Ask God to help you discover what money reveals about your own character. He will help to reveal what's in your heart—good or for bad—and then offer His help if you need it.

Forgiveness

MOST BEAUTIFUL WORD

*[God] has rescued us from the power
of darkness and transferred us into the
kingdom of his beloved Son, in whom we
have redemption, the forgiveness of sins.*
COLOSSIANS 1:13–14 NRSV

Forgiveness. Could there be a more beautiful word in all the English language? Perhaps. But this one should be at the top of the list, for it has taken us from hopelessness and lacking, to fullness of life both now and for the future. Because we are forgiven, we will not receive the fate we deserve but rather, the great and wondrous promises we do not deserve. Our good and loving heavenly Father has forgiven and reconciled us to Himself. Praise His holy name!

FORGIVENESS FREES

Forgive anyone who does you wrong,
just as Christ has forgiven you.
COLOSSIANS 3:13 CEV

Our God has given us a most wonderful gift—the ability to begin again. He has washed away misguided thoughts and behaviors and offered us clean hearts. He has forgiven us, and He asks us to forgive as well. Of course, only God can forgive sin. But we can forgive any trespasses that are made against us. God asks us to work in league with Him—to free others as we have been freed.

Freedom

THE GIFT OF CHOICE

I will sacrifice a voluntary offering to you;
I will praise your name, O LORD, for it is good.
PSALM 54:6 NLT

. . . .

Why would God give us freedom of choice? He must have known the destruction we would bring on ourselves and into the lives of others. But His motivation is clear. Fellowship that is mandated is not fellowship at all, only coerced consent. Much more than creatures who would mindlessly obey, God wanted fellowship with those who would choose to know Him, to love Him, and to live in relationship with Him. What is your choice?

SECOND CHANCES

You have been called to live in freedom, my brothers and sisters. But don't use your freedom to satisfy your sinful nature. Instead, use your freedom to serve one another in love.
GALATIANS 5:13 NLT

. . . .

God has not only given us the power to choose freely but has also released us from the devastating penalty of our poor choices. He knew from the beginning that freedom of choice would make us vulnerable, so He built second chances into the bedrock of His gift. He provided a Savior, who would pay the cost His justice demands, and in turn, free us to choose again. Give thanks today for the precious gift of the Savior.

Friends

A TRUE FRIEND

*Some friends play at friendship but a true
friend sticks closer than one's nearest kin.*
PROVERBS 18:24 NRSV

. . . .

If we listed the characteristics we would expect to
find in a true friend, we would quickly realize that
God has them all. He is always there for us and
committed to our interest. He gives sound advice
and is ever loving. He is loyal, kind, trustworthy,
and forgiving. He always tells us the truth, and when
our feet leave the straight path, He does all He can
to point us back to safety. We can thank Him for
being the truest friend of all.

FRIENDS ALONG THE WAY

*These God-chosen lives all around—
what splendid friends they make!*
PSALM 16:3 MSG

Friendship is a vital element in the lives of most women. Our friends inspire us, comfort us, and listen to us when we need to vent. Friends know all about us, but they love us anyway. They help us keep our heads above water when the floods come. What a wonderful gift friends are! Each day we should bring hearts full of thanks to God for giving us friends to join us on the journey of life.

Future

HOPE FOR THE FUTURE

*I know the thoughts that I think toward you,
says the LORD, thoughts of peace and not
of evil, to give you a future and a hope.*
JEREMIAH 29:11 NKJV

• •

What will the future bring? It's a question we've all asked. We want to know if we have anything to look forward to, a great purpose that will make each day of life worth living. God doesn't lay out the future in front of us, mostly because much of our future is directly related to our choices and how we respond to the circumstances in our lives. God does say, however, that the future He envisions for us is an excellent one.

HEAVENLY FUTURE

Good people can look forward to a bright future.
PROVERBS 13:9 NCV

God doesn't lay out the specifics of our lives before us, but He does tell us that our future extends far past the days we live here on earth. If we are trusting in Him, our future includes a heavenly hope—eternity with our Father God. Our future there will be unfettered by flawed human motivations and abilities. Our heavenly future has been planned from the foundation of the earth and is as certain as God Himself!

Generosity

PURE WATERS

The generous soul will be made rich,
and he who waters will also be watered himself.
PROVERBS 11:25 NKJV

All freshwater lakes have outlets. Without them, the water would become stagnant and brackish. The same is true in our lives. If we only receive and fail to give, we will become subject to greed. We will no longer be satisfied with what we have; instead, it will take more and more to satisfy us. But when we are generous with others, our lives remain in balance, our inner waters pure. We do not become slaves to what God has given, but masters of His goodness.

LEARNING TO SHARE

[Jesus said], "Live generously and graciously toward others, the way God lives toward you."
MATTHEW 5:48 MSG

. . . .

One of the first things a child must learn is to share. Why? Because relationships work only where there is give and take. A person who is selfish and greedy attracts only those like herself. She gives nothing and soon finds herself surrounded by false friends with their own agendas. God shares with us the very best that He has. He urges us to share with those around us. Sharing helps us to experience both compassion and gratitude.

Gentleness

GENTLE SHEPHERD

Your right hand has held me up,
your gentleness has made me great.
PSALM 18:35 NKJV

One of the primary images the Bible gives for Jesus is that of shepherd. He tends to His children as a shepherd tenderly cares for his flock—protecting them from predators, and leading them to good pastures and fresh water as they have need. So often we think of God as harsh and demanding, but His commandments are part of His protective care. Like a shepherd, He works to keep us out of harm's way. He truly is our Gentle Shepherd.

HOW WE TREAT OTHERS

*Let everyone see that you
are gentle and kind.*
PHILIPPIANS 4:5 NCV

. . . .

As human beings, we can sometimes be harsh and unkind. We feel it's important to say how we feel or convince others to see things our way—no matter what. And when we do, we bring dishonor to our God, who is always gentle with us. He does not push His way into our lives. He doesn't bully or coerce. Even though He already knows all, He listens and then gently leads. We can show our gratitude by treating others as He treats us.

Goodness

GOD IS GOOD

[Jesus said], "No one is good but One, that is, God."
MATTHEW 19:17 NKJV

. . . .

For the most part, God is a mystery to us. We simply lack the skills to take in all He has done and all He has said. But this much we can see in everything around us: God is good! Like a good father, He gives everything that is good for us. His intentions behind everything He does for us are good as well. And even when He corrects, He does so for our benefit. God is good—all the time!

NO STRINGS ATTACHED

*How great is your goodness that you
have stored up for those who fear you.*
PSALM 31:19 NCV

• •

Politicians never stop promising us good things,
but what they deliver is most often something
else altogether. That's not the case with our God.
He keeps all His promises as only He can. When
He brings good into our lives, there are no strings
attached. He isn't bargaining for our vote. He does
it because He loves us completely. We can trust in
His goodness always.

God's Love

ONE TRUE LOVE

God's love will continue forever.
PSALM 52:1 NCV

. . . .

We cling to those we love. We dig in deeply and confidently, even though we know that human love often fails. The brightest of romances often go sour. The love of friends sometimes does as well. The love of God is the only sure thing in this world. His perfect love lasts forever. It is the one true and lasting love we can find; and it is His love alone that makes all other love possible. Thank your heavenly Father for His unconditional love today.

THE FACE OF LOVE

Walk in the way of love,
just as Christ loved us.
EPHESIANS 5:2

. . . .

God counts on those who have experienced His love to share it with others. Although He is all around us and His love shows in all He says and does, there are some who cannot hear Him, who cannot see Him. Our human expressions of Christ's love may be all some people see in this world. With grateful hearts, God expects us to pass along His love, to make it known to all we encounter.

God's Mercy

KEPT BY HIS MERCY

The LORD your God is a merciful God.
DEUTERONOMY 4:31

. . . .

We are delicate beings living on a fragile planet. Our survival can only be termed a miracle. Meteors and comets. . .disease and death. . .threats lurk around every corner of our world. And even though we humans are capable of immense evil, God holds us in His hand. His great mercy alone keeps us from complete destruction. We owe Him not only our gratitude but our complete devotion, for we are kept by His mercy and love.

SHARING THE GIFT

*[Jesus said,] "Be merciful just
as your Father is merciful."*
LUKE 6:36

. . . .

The Bible tells the story of a man whose master had mercy on him and forgave his great debt. Clearly the man was ungrateful, for soon after, he refused to show mercy on a man who was indebted to him. Our heavenly Father has shown us His mercy—undeserved and unexpected. We can best show our thankfulness by following His beautiful example. Mercy is a gift—a gift we are asked to share with the world.

God's Purpose

EMPOWERED TO SUCCEED

The plans of the LORD stand firm forever,
the purposes of his heart through all generations.
PSALM 33:11

· ·

God has given each of us free will. He allows us to cut our own paths, make our own choices. His purposes for us are not restrictive, but empowering. Whatever we choose to do, He wants us to be successful, to deal honestly, to fully enjoy the work we have chosen, and most importantly, to honor Him in it. He intends for us to use the gifts and talents He has placed in us and to live our lives to the fullest.

READY TO HELP

Without counsel purposes are disappointed.
PROVERBS 15:22 KJV

. . . .

Each of our lives has purpose and meaning. We are much more than a happy accident. And like any good father, God wants to see us become all we can be. He wants to help us find our highest calling, our most worthwhile pursuits. Sometimes, though, those purposes are hard to sort out. When we don't know which way to go, He is always there to encourage and guide. When we seek Him out, He is always ready to help and lead us in the right direction.

God's Patience

GOD NEVER GIVES UP

*[God] is patient with you, not wanting anyone
to perish, but everyone to come to repentance.*
2 PETER 3:9

. . . .

For most people, patience is hard. Human nature
just doesn't like to wait. Fortunately, God isn't
subject to our all-too-human impulses. He has all
the time in the world. No matter how many times
we mess up, He is always ready to forgive, always
ready to help us get back on track with our lives.
God will never give up on us. We can be thankful
that He waits patiently for us to draw close to Him.

LEARNING TO WAIT

Be completely humble and gentle;
be patient, bearing with one another in love.
EPHESIANS 4:2

. . . .

One of the most difficult things to do is to wait on God, to relax and let Him put the pieces of our lives into place. Like wayward children, we want to do everything for ourselves. We are quick to implement hasty solutions and take unfounded advice, no matter how many times we've already seen that our impatience only serves to make things worse. Thank God. . .His answers are always worth waiting for!

God's Will

ALONG THE WAY

Commit your work to the LORD,
and your plans will be established.
PROVERBS 16:3 NRSV

. . . .

When we head down a new path, wouldn't it be nice if we could look ahead and see everything—good and bad—we will encounter along the way? Being able to anticipate the obstacles would offer quite the advantage, making success much easier to come by. Imagine this: God does see the beginning from the end, and He already knows every step along the way. And it's His will for us to succeed. We can thank Him for guiding us when we cannot always see for ourselves.

CHOOSING THE BEST

Teach me to do your will,
for you are my God.
PSALM 143:10 NRSV

· ·

We all have dreams for our children. We wonder what will spark their passions, what career choices they will make, how they will make their mark on the world. Likewise, our heavenly Father has dreams for us. He hopes we will choose the very best pursuits and purposes for our lives; and He knows what is best for us. But He will not choose for us. We must do that for ourselves. It's up to us to discover that we cannot have a better life than the one in the center of His will.

Grace

WHAT IS GRACE?

He said to me, "My grace is sufficient for you,
for my power is made perfect in weakness."
2 CORINTHIANS 12:9

. . . .

God often calls us to do things that we never knew we were capable of doing. He almost always pushes us beyond our limits, and He does so in order that we might learn to seek Him out and ask for His help. What we call grace is really that part of our lives where God makes up the difference. Grace takes over when our strength fails and God's strength comes to our rescue. Grace is absolutely amazing!

A GOOD OFFER

*How rich is God's grace, which he
has given to us so fully and freely.*
EPHESIANS 1:7–8 NCV

. . . .

Life is not entirely fair—if it were, we would get
what we deserve, rather than God's full and freely
given blessings. Given a choice, who would be
so foolish as to take a stand based on their own
track record? God knows what we're made of. He
understands that we are human beings fraught
with weaknesses and shortcomings. His grace
makes up the difference. It's an offer too good to
refuse.

Guidance

GENTLE SHEPHERD

*I instruct you in the way of wisdom
and lead you along straight paths.*

PROVERBS 4:11

. . . .

Many of us go through life feeling pushed and prodded and pressured. We must get this done, finish that, do what we can here and there. It's exhausting. What a wonderful thing it is to know that God never pushes or pressures us. He guides us, as the Gentle Shepherd of our souls. We may not be able to determine the path ahead of us, but He surely can. And He is always there to show us the way.

LIFE'S JOURNEY

*LORD, tell me your ways. Show me
how to live. Guide me in your truth.*
PSALM 25:4-5 NCV

Navigating this big, media-saturated world is not
easy. Fortunately, we don't have to go it alone.
Our God walks with us every step of the way. The
Bible says that He never leaves our side. What a
wonderful promise that is—our loving, heavenly
Father leading us through every minute of this
journey we call life. It's up to us to listen for His
voice, to follow with our hearts—so we may never
walk alone.

Health

A MASTERFUL CREATION

The Lord cares about our bodies.
1 CORINTHIANS 6:13 NLT

Both tough as nails and gentle as a dove, a woman's body is a masterful creation. It can endure the rigors of childbirth and tenderly caress and care for a fragile newborn. Our bodies, though, don't always function as they should. God expects us to care responsibly for the bodies He has given us, but there will be times when illness and injury are unavoidable. During those times of physical weakness, He asks that we come to Him, the Great Creator, and ask for His healing touch.

EMOTIONAL BEINGS

A heart of peace gives life to the body.
PROVERBS 14:30

. . . .

We women are emotional beings. God created us that way so we would be able to function well as wives and mothers. Unfortunately, we tend to pay less attention to our emotional health than we do our physical health. In order to be at our best, our emotions should not rage out of control; nor should they keep us preoccupied. Thankfully, God is always ready to set us right when we are faithful to ask Him.

Holiness

PERFECT IN GOODNESS

"There is no one holy like the LORD."
1 SAMUEL 2:2

. . . .

The word *holy* sounds kind of old and religious, doesn't it? But its true meaning is always relevant. It means to be perfect in goodness. And that's what God is. . .perfect in His goodness to us. He doesn't coddle or spoil us. He doesn't neglect or withhold from us. He isn't overcome by emotion. Nor is He rigid and stern, without feeling. He is the perfect Father—always there for us, always committed to our good.

LIVING A BLESSED LIFE

God did not call us to be impure,
but to live a holy life.
1 THESSALONIANS 4:7

. . . .

Why does God judge one thing to be good and holy, while He calls other things unholy? Are His judgments random and arbitrary? God looks not only at the action itself but also at the consequence of the action. We might judge love to always be good, but when we act on love outside of marriage, for example, the consequence is often hurt and despair for ourselves and others. God's laws are protective in nature. A holy life is a blessed life.

Holy Spirit

ONE GOD

*In the beginning, God created the heavens
and the earth. . . . And the Spirit of God
was hovering over the waters.*

GENESIS 1:1–2

. . . .

Some have wondered if we worship three Gods—
the Father, the Son, and the Holy Spirit. It's simple
semantics, really. We serve one God and only one—
but He has three distinct roles in our lives. He is
our Creator, our Savior, and the One who inspires
us and moves in our hearts. Just like we, as women,
also have many roles—daughter, wife, mother. . .
for example. We can be thankful that in all these
ways, He is our one true God.

IN HIS PRESENCE

In the same way, the Spirit
helps us in our weakness.
ROMANS 8:26

. . . .

A popular song tells us that God watches us from a distance. But He does so much more than that. His Holy Spirit dwells right here with us, in us, and around us. He hears our innermost thoughts and knows our silent pain. Because He is here, we are never alone—never without His comfort, guidance, and inspiration. Because He is here, we can know Him up close and personal. Thankfully, we are always in His presence.

Hope

HOPE IS AN ANCHOR

*We have this hope as an anchor
for the soul, firm and secure.*
HEBREWS 6:19

. . . .

Hope doesn't "float." It is the steady, rock-solid foundation for everything we do in life. It is the reason we continue on, the reason our lives have meaning and purpose. When people no longer care. . .no longer have the will to live. . .don't we say that they have lost all hope? When we place our hope in God, we are strengthened and inspired. Thank Him today for the hope He brings that makes life worth living.

HOPE IN GOD

He shall strengthen your heart,
all you who hope in the LORD.
PSALM 31:24 NKJV

. . . .

What does it mean to "hope in God"? Is it as some have imagined—all of us eventually floating around on clouds, playing harps? We can be certain that God has much more in store for us than that. Our hope begins with eternal life and continues on with never-ending fellowship with God and the fulfillment of all He has created us to be. As the hymn writer, Thomas Chisholm, said, "Peace for today and bright hope for tomorrow!"

Humility

A COSTLY MISTAKE

Humble yourselves, therefore,
under God's mighty hand,
that he may lift you up in due time.
1 PETER 5:6

. . . .

We've all met people who think they know it all.
It's impossible to tell these people anything. Their
refusal to admit their limitations and learn from
others is a costly mistake. When we put up walls
and close our minds to instruction, we make errors—
lots of them. And along with each error comes an
undesired consequence. Humility opens our ears to
hear the truth—and our faithful God always wants
to see us succeed.

ALL GOD'S RESOURCES

All of you be subject one to another,
and be clothed with humility.
1 PETER 5:5 KJV

The one thing pride does very well is alienate us
from others. It causes us to think that we don't need
anyone else in our lives. The tendency to isolate is
why pride so successfully dooms us to failure. But
humility has just the opposite effect. It opens us
up to new ideas and ways of doing things. Humility
allows us to identify the resources of wisdom and
experience God has given us. How can we neglect
to be thankful to such a wonderful God?

Jesus Christ

WHO IS HE?

Jesus replied, "Blessed are you, Simon son of Jonah, for this was not revealed to you by flesh and blood, but by my Father in heaven."
MATTHEW 16:17

. . . .

Jesus asked His disciples to tell Him who they thought He was. At first they just recited what they'd already heard from others, but finally they got down to it. Simon Peter answered Him, "You are the Messiah, the Son of the living God." Before any spiritual journey can begin, that question must be answered: "Who is Jesus to you?" Is He just some historical figure or Bible character? Or is He the Savior, the Messiah, the Son of God?

THE RISEN SAVIOR

"Don't be alarmed," he said, "You are looking for Jesus the Nazarene, who was crucified. He has risen! He is not here."

MARK 16:6

• •

There is a wonderful place in Jerusalem called the "Garden Tomb." Many historians say it is the place where the body of Jesus was placed after His crucifixion. It fits all the criteria, but no one really knows for sure. Why the uncertainty? Simple. The stone burial vault is empty. Some religions worship statues of stone and wood; others worship leaders whose bodies are decaying away in the grave. But Jesus Christ alone is risen from the dead! Rejoice!

Joy

JOY VERSUS HAPPINESS

I will greatly rejoice in the LORD,
my soul shall be joyful in my God.
ISAIAH 61:10 NKJV

. . . .

The Bible urges us to rejoice always. But we often wonder how God expects us to be joyful when things are going wrong all around us. It's purely a matter of definition. Happiness is what we feel in good times, but that sense of happiness disappears when we encounter bad times. Joy, on the other hand, is a constant that resides deep down inside us—in good times and bad. It is born of hope that our Father God has everything under control, and He is riding out the storms right along with us.

IN ALL CIRCUMSTANCES

Rejoice always, pray continually,
give thanks in all circumstances.
1 Thessalonians 5:16–18

. . . .

What does it mean to rejoice always? Does it mean we must smile at all times? Not at all. Joy, unlike happiness, is an inner sense of well-being unrelated to our circumstances. It is inspired by the understanding that our fate is secure, no matter what might come our way. It is choosing to see the big picture, even in the midst of suffering. Joy comes when we decide to hang on to God and constantly praise Him for His presence in our lives.

Justice

WAITING FOR HIM

Many seek an audience with a ruler,
but it is from the LORD that man gets justice.
PROVERBS 29:26

. . . .

A longing for justice is part of the God-seed placed inside us at Creation. We sense it when we see a wrong done—especially when an innocent person is harmed. What we must remember, though, is that God's justice is perfect because He has all the facts. We fall short in that category. When we perceive something to be unjust, it's important for us to go to God with our concerns before we act. The outcome is always best when we wait for God's instructions first.

TRIUMPHING OVER INJUSTICE

What does the LORD require of you?
To act justly and to love mercy and
to walk humbly with your God.

MICAH 6:8

. . . .

Justice is important to God. It's one of the three things He mentions when He tells us what He requires of His children. We are often helpless to right the wrongs we see every day, but we are empowered when it comes to living our own lives in a just manner. Rather than becoming obsessed with injustice, we can overcome it by doing what our Savior calls us to do. We can give thanks to our wise God for showing us how to triumph in an often unjust world.

Kindness

LEARNING KINDNESS

When the kindness and love of God our Savior
appeared, he saved us, not because of righteous
things we had done, but because of his mercy.
TITUS 3:4-5

Imagine what the world would be like if everyone were kind. Such a simple concept, and yet it eludes us. We can, however, choose kindness as the norm in our homes. We can teach it and preach it and practice it, regardless of whether our home is occupied by one or many. So what does kindness look like? Our good God has given us His example. With thankful hearts, we can learn kindness from Him.

THE GIFT OF KINDNESS

*To your service for God, add kindness for
your brothers and sisters in Christ;
and to this kindness, add love.*
2 PETER 1:7 NCV

. . . .

We serve a God who is kind; and when we are kind,
we demonstrate that we are like Him. No wonder
our kind acts not only bless Him, but ourselves and
others as well. It multiplies exponentially. In fact,
to fully understand the potential of kindness, we
must see it first as a gift, unearned and undeserved,
just as God has bestowed it to us. As we are kind
to others, we show our thankfulness for all His
kindness.

Knowledge

APPLICATION

Knowledge of the Holy One is understanding.
PROVERBS 9:10

. . . .

The human brain—much like a computer—is capable of storing enormous quantities of data. But knowledge is more than just facts. True knowledge includes the skill of application. For example, how does the information you've learned about history help you decide who to vote for? The same is true with God. You can never really know Him until you have applied what you think you know about Him to your life. When you come to know Him in this way, you'll have so much more to thank Him for.

REWARDED FOR KNOWLEDGE

*God, who said, "Let light shine out of darkness,"
made his light shine in our hearts to give us
the light of the knowledge of God's glory
displayed in the face of Christ.*

2 CORINTHIANS 4:6

. . . .

In school we are held responsible for what we don't know. We are tested and penalized for wrong answers. But God does things differently. He holds us responsible for what we do know. He rewards us for every layer of knowledge or insight we have concerning Him. The more we know, the more we trust Him. The more we know, the more we love Him. The more we know, the more we recognize His goodness to us. Praise Him!

Laughter

A LAUGHING MATTER

*[God] will yet fill your mouth with laughter
and your lips with shouts of joy.*
JOB 8:21

. . . .

Laughter is amazing. It relieves the stress of every-day life and releases endorphins and adrenaline in our bodies, resulting in a natural high. It has also been shown to improve creativity and enhance memory. And that's not all! Laughter also helps us view ourselves differently, unlocks our minds, and makes us more innovative. Not everything is a laughing matter, but we can thank God for giving us this wonderful outlet for the joy we feel inside.

DOES GOD LAUGH?

A merry heart makes a cheerful countenance.
PROVERBS 15:13 NKJV

. . . .

Nowhere in the Bible does it say that God laughs, but it's a fair assumption. After all, we laugh, and the Bible says we were created in His image. It's also easy to imagine that God likes to see us laugh—especially in the midst of adversity, pain, and hardship. He knows that it strengthens us physically and mentally. Thank God for His faithfulness by regularly exercising laughter in both the good and the not-so-good circumstances of life.

Life

ACCOUNTABLE

Peace of mind means a healthy body.
PROVERBS 14:30 NCV

. . . .

God has given each of us a life to live. Though we honor others through our lives, we alone are held accountable for what we do with the lives we have been given. When we stand before God, the great Creator, we can't make excuses by blaming our parents, our spouses, our employers, our children, our friends, or our government. God has given each of us the power to live our lives to the fullest.

BACK IN THE GAME

*Train yourself to be godly. For physical training
is of some value, but godliness has value
for all things, holding promise for both
the present life and the life to come.*

1 TIMOTHY 4:7-8

. . . .

Too often we fail to thank God for the gift of life.
Instead we complain about finances, physical
limitations, lack of education and opportunities,
uncertain times, and adverse circumstances. These
things do not define us. They are simply obstacles
to be overcome with God's help. Thankful hearts
put us back in the game and help us to become all
God created us to be.

Love

GOD IS LOVE

These three remain: faith, hope and love.
But the greatest of these is love.
Follow the way of love.
1 Corinthians 13:13, 14:1

. . . .

If we were to say that any one characteristic is uniquely God, it would be love. Not only does God do everything He does out of a heart of love, but He instructs us to do the same. Love motivates us to care about others and to put the needs of others ahead of our own. One day we will live in God's kingdom—a kingdom ruled by love. Until then, we can thank Him for loving us by passing that same love on to the lives we touch each day.

REAL LOVE

Dear friends, let us love one another,
for love comes from God. Everyone who loves
has been born of God and knows God.
1 JOHN 4:7–8

· ·

Because we live in a world wrecked by sin, nothing we experience here on earth is truly pure or perfect—nothing that is, but love. Love is the one thing that has overcome sin, afforded forgiveness, and brought Light into our lives. Love is the God-force in our world. It heals and transforms. There is an abundance of flimsy imitations that masquerade as love. But somehow we all know real love when we see it, and we should never settle for less.

Mistakes

TRANSFORMED MISTAKES

Teach us to number our days,
that we may gain a heart of wisdom.
PSALM 90:12

We all make mistakes—some more consequential than others. It would be wonderful if we could ensure all our actions and choices would be spot on; but we human beings don't always do the right thing. When we are suffering as the result of an error in judgment, it's good to know that God never wastes our sorrows. He takes our mistakes and hands them back to us in the form of wisdom and experience.

WHAT'S BEST

We ask God to give you complete
knowledge of his will and to give you
spiritual wisdom and understanding.
COLOSSIANS 1:9 NLT

. . . .

Most of the mistakes we make aren't really mistakes at all. Rather, they are attempts to prove to ourselves that we have a better idea of what's best for us than God does. That's right. . . we think we know better than the One who created us, who knows us inside and out, the One who sees our lives laid out from beginning to end. It is always shortsighted to go against the wisdom and counsel of God—for His counsel is there to protect us from ourselves.

Nature

OUR AMAZING HOME

This is the history of the heavens and the earth
when they were created, in the day that the
LORD God made the earth and the heavens.

GENESIS 2:4 NKJV

. . . .

Now that we are able to see close-up photos of other
planets, we have a better appreciation for the lovely
place God prepared for us here on earth. We take
for granted that there is air to breathe and soil in
which to grow crops. Earth is teeming with life, while
other planets are barren and uninhabitable. Some
say it's just our good fortune. But we know better.
Each time we look at our natural surroundings, we
have an opportunity to give thanks to God for our
amazing home.

GOD'S DOING

Take a good look at God's wonders—
they'll take your breath away.
PSALM 66:5 MSG

. . . .

Some people insist that the beautiful and unique creations that surround us here on earth are accidents, the fortunate result of time and evolution. What a far-fetched assumption! All that variety and attention to detail could only have come from our God, whose intelligence and creativity are beyond the limitations of our human minds. The beauty we see in nature is God's masterpiece, and He alone deserves our thanks.

Peace

AN AMAZING GIFT

Christ Himself is our peace.
EPHESIANS 2:14 NCV

. . . .

On the occasion of Christ's birth, the angels sang, "Peace on earth, good will toward men!" It's a glorious declaration, but what kind of peace were the heavenly hosts announcing? After all, wars abound, human relations are chaotic, and inner peace is much sought after and rarely realized. So what exactly were the angels celebrating? God sent His Son to establish peace between us and our Creator. Jesus made it possible for us to know our heavenly Father. What an amazing gift of peace!

PEACE AND QUIET

*May the Lord of peace himself give
you peace at all times in all ways.
The Lord be with all of you.*
2 Thessalonians 3:16 nrsv

No matter how hard we try to block it out, the world around us is blaring with man-made chatter and activity. No wonder we often confuse peace with quiet. We want to give our weary minds a rest. Peace and quiet are not interchangeable, however. Peace refers to a lack of struggle, an end to hostilities, a settled state of mind. Thanks to our loving Creator, we can have peace in the very midst of this noisy, chaotic world.

Persecution

OUR PERSECUTORS

*I tell you: love your enemies and pray for
those who persecute you, that you may
be children of your Father in heaven.*
MATTHEW 5:44-45

. . . .

We tend to see others' differing opinions as
indictments of our own. So it should be no surprise
that those who don't share our faith in God may
sometimes treat us unkindly or even with contempt.
No wonder Jesus says we should pray for those
who wrong us. They are striking out from the
barrenness of their own hearts. Let us thank God
for our persecutors, and ask Him to touch each one
of their hearts with His love and mercy.

THE FAITHLESS ONES

*All have sinned and fall short of the glory of God,
and all are justified freely by his grace through
the redemption that came by Christ Jesus.*
ROMANS 3:23-24

. . . .

We all know what it feels like to be wronged, but
rarely do we realize that we are sometimes guilty of
wronging others as well. When we treat those who
don't share our faith with disdain, we are plainly
demonstrating that our personal faith is not entirely
strong and secure. If our faith were more certain,
we would have no reason to feel threatened by the
lack of faith we see in others. We should always
give thanks for the faithless ones God has placed in
our lives—for we once walked in their shoes.

Perseverance

WHAT DOESN'T COME EASY

*You must hold on, so you can do what God
wants and receive what he has promised.*
HEBREWS 10:36 NCV

· ·

We live in a fast-paced electronic world, where most
everything comes quickly and easily. It's really quite
wonderful. But on the flip side, we've lost something
in the process—the art of persevering. If the desired
result doesn't come quickly, we move on. *Why
bother?* we think. This is unfortunate, because many
of life's greatest treasures are secured only through
patience and struggle and perseverance. Thank
God today for those things that haven't come easily—
for those things that have stretched your faith.

MY DESIRE OR HIS?

Take delight in the LORD, and he will
give you the desires of your heart.
PSALM 37:4

How do we know when to persevere and when to place our focus on something else and stop hoping for something that will never happen? When the struggle seems to be overwhelming, we must ask God, "Is this objective part of Your plan or my own?" No doubt, some of our desires are better left unfulfilled. Asking the heavenly Father to reveal His will for our lives releases us from futile effort, and it strengthens our resolve to persevere for the things God Himself has placed in our hearts.

Perspective

LESSONS OF PERSPECTIVE

"My thoughts are not your thoughts, neither are your ways my ways," declares the LORD.

ISAIAH 55:8-9

. . . .

We've all been a witness to lessons on perspective. For example, we can't rightly comprehend an elephant by only handling its trunk. Truthfully, perspective is often complicated. It's distorted by our experience—both great and small—by what we've been taught, and how we've responded to life so far. Thank God for bringing the full, pure and simple truth to our lives and for helping us to align our perspective with His. It won't happen overnight, but He will help us stay on the narrow path.

THE WAYS OF GOD

All the ways of the LORD
are loving and faithful.
PSALM 25:10

We've all looked back into our past and realized that, at one time or another, something painful in our lives turned out to be fortuitous—bringing some unexpected blessing, or even changing the entire course of our lives for the better. We sheepishly recall lashing out in a difficult time, unaware of what God really had in store for us. Take heart. God won't allow suffering into our lives without some greater purpose. When we are hurting, we must thank God for seeing what we do not. We would be wise to trust His perspective—always.

Praise

ALMIGHTY GOD

Sing to [the LORD], sing praise to him;
tell of all his wonderful acts.
1 CHRONICLES 16:9

. . . .

We all like to be praised—especially when it comes from those we love, or those we go the extra mile for. God likes to hear our praise as well. Although He can see that we appreciate the blessings He pours out on our lives, He still likes to hear us speak the words. We should pause often to praise God for the mighty things He's done for us, for His presence in our lives, and the hope we have for the future.

PRAISING OTHERS

The LORD takes delight in his people;
he crowns the humble with victory.

PSALM 149:4

• •

Like God, human beings respond to praise in a positive way. In fact, praise has proven just as effective as threats, promises, or any other incentive, and perhaps even more so. God is good, so let us praise the good things we see in those around us. Let us strive to emphasize the positive instead of the negative. There will always be times when we must speak the truth in love, but it is better received by a heart built with praise.

Prayer

HE IS NEAR

The LORD is near to all who call on him,
to all who call on him in truth.
PSALM 145:18

• •

Prayer is often thought to be a complex, multi-layered activity. When it comes to prayer, we wonder if we're worthy. . .if we're speaking the proper words . . .if we're in the right place. . . just to name a few of the questions we ask ourselves. To put it simply, prayer is nothing more than conversation with God—so any questions we ask ourselves should be directly related to our relationship with Him. It's often awkward to converse with someone we don't know. But once we get to know our heavenly Father, prayer will come easily.

HE IS LISTENING

You must keep praying. Keep watching!
Be thankful always.
COLOSSIANS 4:2 NCV

. . . .

Our God is more great and mighty than our feeble human minds could ever imagine. No wonder we question how to properly speak to Him. But, amazingly, we have been welcomed into God's inner court, invited to speak as we see fit, and promised that when we do, He will always be listening. This is clearly beyond our comprehension, and yet it's true. Our hearts should always be full of thanks for our heavenly Father's welcoming arms.

Priorities

HUMAN NATURE

We fix our eyes not on what is seen,
but on what is unseen, since what is seen
is temporary, but what is unseen is eternal.
2 CORINTHIANS 4:18

. . . .

Even the person who says she has no priorities really does. We automatically prioritize those things that make us feel good. When someone says she doesn't have time or money for something, that person sometimes means she doesn't choose to use her resources in that way. That's just human nature, and it means we need to review our priorities regularly to ensure that they line up with God's. Otherwise, our lives won't count for much. Ask God to help you get your priorities in order today.

PURPOSEFUL CHOICES

*We are His workmanship, created in Christ
Jesus for good works, which God prepared
beforehand that we should walk in them.*
EPHESIANS 2:10 NKJV

. . . .

We've all heard someone say, "You'd better check
your priorities." But what does it mean? Priorities
are purposeful choices. They give us the ability
to move out of default mode and into choosing to
do things that we know have meaning. Without
priorities, we are subject to detours, roadblocks,
delays, and distractions. God wants us to have
our priorities straight—to know what we should
be doing and then take action. He wants us to live
with purpose.

Promises

GOD'S PROMISES

The LORD is trustworthy in all he promises and faithful in all he does.

PSALM 145:13

. . . .

At one time or another, we've all made promises we didn't keep, despite our good intentions. But God keeps His promises—every one, all the time! Depending on how they are interpreted, there are between 3,000 and 5,000 promises in the Bible. These promises represent the remarkable treasure we share when we walk in relationship with our generous and loving heavenly Father. Even when we aren't cognizant, God's promises clear the path before us. Our part is simply to say thank You!

TRUSTING IN PROMISES

*My eyes stay open through the watches of the
night, that I may meditate on your promises.*
PSALM 119:148

. . . .

Who do we cling to when times are tough? We
receive some comfort from family and friends, of
course. Or we can reach down deep inside and
access our own inner strength. We can even put
our trust in politicians and government leaders. In
the final evaluation, though, only God's promises
can be trusted. The path to His promises is often
shrouded in unknowns, but we can know with
certainty that God will never leave us, even on
our darkest days.

Prosperity

LIVING GOD'S WAY

Keep my commands in your heart,
for they will prolong your life many years
and bring you peace and prosperity.
PROVERBS 3:1–2

· ·

Many speak critically about God's laws. They feel it's a personal affront that God issued commands. *Who is He to tell us how to live?* they think. These people are missing the motive behind His commands. They are not arbitrary rulings of an arrogant deity, but rather guidelines for living fully—guidelines given by a loving heavenly Father. Even when we don't fully understand God's purpose, we can be sure that keeping His commandments leads to prosperous, happy lives.

OUR KING

Let the LORD be magnified, which hath
pleasure in the prosperity of his servant.
PSALM 35:27 KJV

· ·

Very few earthly kings care about the prosperity of
those who live within their kingdoms. Many kings
live in opulence while giving little notice to the
needs of their citizens. Not so in the kingdom of
God. God delights in blessing those who choose
to live under His banner. Our welfare is of utmost
concern to Him. And He isn't just concerned with
meeting our physical needs. He showers us with
blessings of every kind, more than we can count,
so much more than we deserve.

Provision

GIVING GOD'S WAY

Giving God's Way God will generously provide all you need. Then you will always have everything you need and plenty left over to share with others.
2 CORINTHIANS 9:8 NLT

. . . .

How does God provide for us? Does He drop pennies from heaven or alter bank records to show more money in our accounts? No, God uses people. He instructs us to reach out to others and share what we have. And when we are the ones in need, He asks others to share with us. The Bible tells us that we should give to others freely and generously, with a grateful and cheerful heart. Give thanks to the heavenly Father for His generosity through the willing hearts of others.

RELY ON HIM

My God will fully satisfy every need of yours
according to his riches in glory in Christ Jesus.
PHILIPPIANS 4:19 NRSV

• •

Many times we limit God's provision by asking Him to provide only for our physical needs. But He wants to provide so much more. He wants us to be strong and healthy in every aspect of our lives—physically, emotionally, and spiritually. His provision keeps us emotionally centered and spiritually astute. His provision soothes our emotions and comforts us in loss. In every way, we can thank Him for seeing that we have all we need.

Quietness

A QUIET PLACE

"Be still, and know that I am God;
I will be exalted among the nations,
I will be exalted in the earth."

PSALM 46:10

. . . .

Most of us spend our days in busy households and workplaces. So much for quietness! That's why it's essential to find a quiet place where we can go from time to time. This should be a calming environment where we can focus ourselves fully in thought and prayer, renewing our stress-filled minds and bodies. We should not feel guilty about taking this time for ourselves. We're at our best when we've had time to focus on God and allow Him to soothe our ruffled feathers.

HIS VOICE

I have calmed and quieted myself,
I am like a weaned child with its mother;
like a weaned child I am content.
PSALM 131:2

Taking time to quiet our hearts and minds allows us to think more clearly, make better choices, and gain control of our emotions. Quiet time should serve one additional purpose: it should be a time when we take extra care to listen for God's voice. His words to us, no matter how few, are truth and life. They calm, heal, and clarify. They are filled with comfort and encouragement. Anything is possible when we take time to be tuned in to God.

Reason

FAITH AND REASON

*"Come now, let us settle
the matter," says the LORD.*
ISAIAH 1:18

. . . .

We sometimes have the notion that faith and reason are incompatible. But, in fact, the power to reason is one of the abilities that makes us most like God. Faith doesn't negate our intelligence, rather it expands it. God expects us to have questions. Of course, there are many things that are beyond our understanding, but God allows—even encourages—us to search out answers to life's questions. He wouldn't have it any other way.

THE BEGINNING AND THE END

*The one who cherishes
understanding will soon prosper.*
PROVERBS 19:8

. . . .

As we live out our faith, there will be times when we understand what is going on around us. We really "get it." But there will be other times when we must move forward, trusting that God has His own purpose in mind. There is a reason behind God's plan, even when we aren't able to figure it all out. When we come to these places, we must remember that God knows all things—the end from the beginning and everything in between—and we can take great comfort in that.

Reconciliation

100 PERCENT SETTLED

All this is from God, who reconciled us
to himself through Christ and gave
us the ministry of reconciliation.
2 CORINTHIANS 5:18

. . . .

The word reconcile has a number of meanings. For example, we reconcile our checkbooks. In this case, the word means "to line up, settle, or make to agree." When we speak of reconciliation with God, it carries the notion that we must settle our differences. Unlike any of our human relationships, we were 100 percent wrong and God did 100 percent of the work to make us 100 percent right again. He fully reconciled us to Himself.

JOY OF RELEASE

As far as it depends on you,
live at peace with everyone.
ROMANS 12:18

. . . .

Most of us live our lives with unresolved issues—hurts that haven't healed, relationships left broken, wrongs never righted. They litter our emotional landscape and leave us feeling undone. Of course, we can't allow ourselves to obsess over situations that are far beyond our control. But we should make every effort, with God's help, to clean up those unpleasant corners of our lives when we can. And even when our efforts are refused, we can feel the sweet joy of release.

Redemption

WE ARE REDEEMED!

You know that it was not with perishable things such as silver or gold that you were redeemed from the empty way of life handed down to you from your ancestors, but with the precious blood of Christ, a lamb without blemish or defect.

1 PETER 1:18–19

. . . .

A pawn shop is a "house of redemption." That's right. All day long, people enter pawn shops to offer up their valuables for cash. Then later, they come and buy their items back or redeem them. While God didn't offer us up for cash, He gave us the gift of free will. And thinking we could have more and be more, we sold ourselves. That might have been the end of it. But God paid the very dear price to free us. We are redeemed!

PAYING THE PRICE

You came near when I called you,
and you said, "Do not fear." You, Lord,
took up my case; you redeemed my life.
LAMENTATIONS 3:57–58

• •

Though we are in need of redemption, we cannot redeem ourselves. We are helpless until someone comes along and pays the amount required for our release. We cannot redeem ourselves through good works. The price for our lives was far too high, and one that only God Himself could pay. Our redemption was secured with the blood of One without sin, perfect and undefiled, and standing in our place. We can thank God for paying the price through the blood of our Lord Jesus.

Relationships

THE PERFECT ANSWER

I will receive you. And will be a Father unto you, and ye shall be my sons and daughters, saith the Lord Almighty.
2 CORINTHIANS 6:17-18 KJV

• •

Many people know about God, but they don't realize that they can live in relationship with Him. Imagine having almighty God in your circle of friends— talking to Him, spending time with Him day after day. God has made it possible for each of us to be in relationship with Him. Because we could never reach up to Him, He has reached down to us. We don't have to find God. He has already found us. All we have to do is take His hand and smile.

FAITHFUL ONES

Be devoted to one another in love.
Honor one another above yourselves.
ROMANS 12:10

. . . .

Certainly there are those among us who would willingly exile themselves to a deserted island and be perfectly content there. But most of us need vital contact with other human beings. We need the opportunity to share our joys and sorrows, our blessings and pain, with other human beings. We feel the need to love and be loved. Give thanks to God for faithful friends and family, those special people who keep us smiling and loving and caring.

Repentance

WHEN WE REPENT

Whenever anyone turns to the Lord, the veil is taken away. Now the Lord is the Spirit, and where the Spirit of the Lord is, there is freedom.

2 CORINTHIANS 3:16–17

. . . .

Someone you love is walking away from you, and soon you won't be able to see him or her at all. But you call out that person's name. "Come back," you say. "All is forgiven!" Hearing your invitation, your loved one turns and runs toward you. Oh, the joy! That's exactly what happens when we repent. Instead of walking away from God, we are running to Him. And He waits with open arms, longing to hold us in His loving embrace.

FREE WILL

*This is what the LORD says: "If you repent,
I will restore you that you may serve me."*
JEREMIAH 15:19

. . . .

When God invested free will into the hearts of
mankind, He took a big risk. He knew that, given the
choice, some would reject Him. Yet He took that risk
for our sake—for the sake of those who would choose
to love Him in return, those who would be delighted
to walk with Him day after day. Repentance doesn't
mean giving up our way. It means turning from the
things that separate us from God, so that we might
live in constant fellowship with Him.

Respect

SHOWING RESPECT

Those who respect the LORD will have security.
PROVERBS 14:26 NCV

. . . .

Where there is no respect, there will be no thankfulness. The two are mutually exclusive. When we show respect, we are acknowledging that someone has brought value to our lives. When we show respect for God, we are acknowledging His goodness to us. When we respect our parents, we are acknowledging what they have done for us. Respect leads to thankfulness, and thankfulness keeps us safe from the destructive forces of pride and vanity.

LOVING OURSELVES

Do not be shaped by this world; instead be changed within by a new way of thinking.
ROMANS 12:2 NCV

- -

We've all known people who seem to have no respect for anyone or anything. We find them repulsive; but in truth, those people are lashing out. While they may be defaming others, the deficit is all theirs. Such people see themselves as worthless, without value. Were they to know the depth of God's love for them, His plan and design for their lives, they would behave differently. Only when we respect ourselves can we respect others.

Rest

STOP AND CONSIDER

[God] rested on the seventh day
from all His work which He had done.
GENESIS 2:2 NKJV

. . . .

The Bible says that on the seventh day, after He had created the heavens and the earth, God rested. Are we to believe that God was tired? Not likely. Perhaps this time of rest was to enjoy the work of His own hands. We all need rest for our physical bodies, especially considering the day-to-day responsibilities we face. But rest also means to stop, look around, and consider the wonders in our lives. We can thank our heavenly Father for providing a precedent to slow down and rest!

PLANNED PAUSES

Return to your rest, my soul,
for the LORD has been good to you.
PSALM 116:7

In musical terms, a rest is a pause—a brief, planned event. Without it, the music would become monotonous, even hurried and chaotic. With it, the listener can rightly appreciate all the notes that come before and after. God has planned for times of rest in our lives—pauses necessary for healing, for reflection, for change of direction. . . Without them our lives become unbalanced. With them, our lives sing with wholeness and harmony.

Responsibility

COME UNTO ME

[Jesus said to his disciples,] "Come to me, all you that are weary and are carrying heavy burdens, and I will give you rest."
MATTHEW 11:28 NRSV

Remember the old adage that says a woman's work is never done? Newsflash: it's true! Our lives revolve around the needs of others; and for the most part, we carry those responsibilities without question. It's just what we do. It sure is comforting to know that we aren't alone in it, though. God is always there, watching for things we cannot see and strengthening us when we feel we can't take one more step. Without Him, our loads would be more than we could bear.

JUST SAY NO

All must carry their own loads.
GALATIANS 6:5 NRSV

• •

Because women carry so much day-to-day responsibility, it's easy for us to feel the weight of burdens that aren't even our own. There are times when no is the absolute best answer. Taking on too much can distract us from our legitimate responsibilities; it can leave us physically and emotionally drained—no good to ourselves or anyone else; and we slight others when we take on the tasks God meant for them to tackle. Ask God to help you say no when necessary. He'll give you the courage you need!

Revelation

TRUE INSIGHT

This is my prayer, that your love may overflow more and more with knowledge and full insight to help you to determine what is best.
PHILIPPIANS 1:9–10 NRSV

. . . .

Most of us think of revelation in terms of grandiose future events. But every woman has need of revelation in her everyday life. . .maybe to illuminate a deeper walk with God or solve a sticky family situation. We try to be vigilant, to do our homework, but we live in a world of smoke and mirrors. God has promised to give us insight when we need it, to reveal what is true and good. What a wonderful God we serve!

GOD'S BOOK

I have more insight than all my teachers,
for I meditate on your statutes.
PSALM 119:99

. . . .

In our world, there remains one great source of insight and revelation. It is the book that God gave us—the Bible. Over the course of time, it has sustained its ability to provide wisdom, insight, and revelation concerning how best to live our lives. It has often been described as a road map from God, to God, and about God. Much more than just words on a page, the Bible offers revelation that resonates with the Spirit of God.

Righteousness

SIMPLY PUT

The work of righteousness shall be peace;
and the effect of righteousness quietness
and assurance for ever.
ISAIAH 32:17 KJV

• •

Righteousness is one of those big words that we
sometimes find intimidating. Although its definition
lies very near the surface, we might be reluctant
to guess its meaning. Very simply, righteousness
means "consistently doing what is right." Whenever
we come across that word, we can insert those few
simple words in its place. Forget about situational
ethics, God has set a standard for right and wrong.
It's a standard He lives by Himself.

PLEASING TO GOD

*The path of the righteous is like the morning sun,
shining ever brighter till the full light of day.*
PROVERBS 4:18

. . . .

A young duo finished their act to thunderous applause, and then someone called out, "Righteous, brothers!" The name stuck, and many years later, we still know them as the Righteous Brothers. In this case, the listener meant that the sound was clear and harmonious. . .pleasing to the ear. When we live righteously, our lives become harmonious with intentions to live a full life pleasing to God, to whom we rightly give our thanks and praise.

Sacrifice

UNSUNG SACRIFICES

*I urge, you, brothers and sisters, in view
of God's mercy, to offer your bodies as a
living sacrifice, holy and pleasing to God—
this is your spiritual worship.*

ROMANS 12:1

• •

Women instinctively give of themselves to others—
their children, their spouses, their parents, their
friends. . . We know how to step up and do what
needs to be done, no matter the cost. Sadly those
sacrifices often go unsung, but God always sees
what we do for others. He understands, because
He set the standard for sacrifice by giving Himself fully for us. When the time is right, He will
reward us accordingly.

THE NATURE OF SACRIFICE

*Do not forget to do good and
to share with others, for with
such sacrifices God is pleased.*
HEBREWS 13:16

. . . .

What is the difference between a good deed and a
sacrifice? One is an action; the other an exchange.
Our actions become sacrificial when they demand
that we give up something, when we put others
before ourselves, when we forego our own interests for the interests of others. Like love, sacrifice
is part of God's nature. When we live sacrificial
lives, we honor our heavenly Father and show that
He lives in us.

Scriptures

GOD'S WORDS

He [Jesus] opened their understanding,
that they might comprehend the Scriptures.
LUKE 24:45 NKJV

. . . .

The Bible is not just another book. It's holy, because the words of the Bible weren't crafted by some clever wordsmith. Rather, they were given to men by revelation from God; therefore, they are holy words, God's words. Some have tried to make light of the holy nature of the Bible, but its amazing symmetry, wisdom, and beauty over the course of thousands of years cannot otherwise be explained. Thank God today for sending us His words.

THE WORD OF GOD

God has breathed life into all of Scripture. It is useful for teaching us what is true. . .for correcting our mistakes. . .for making our lives whole again.
2 TIMOTHY 3:16 NIRV

. . . .

We know the Bible is filled with God's words, but what is the overall nature of this holy document? The Bible tells the story of God's interactions with mankind, from the first breath of life to the last. It tells us who God is and what He expects of us. It is a love story, a history lesson, a creative masterpiece, and an inspired document filled with timeless truths. Thank God for the life it brings to those who take His Word to heart!

Service

THE GIFT OF SERVING

Serve wholeheartedly, as if you were serving the Lord, not people, because you know that the Lord will reward each are for whatever good they do.
EPHESIANS 6:7-8

. . . .

God's Word tells us that service is a gift given by God Himself for the good of His people. We've all known those who have received such a gift. They seem to always be quietly helping others, away from the spotlight, content to serve without fanfare. They aren't motivated by pride, need, or praise. Instead, they see serving others as a way to serve God. Let's thank Him for this special gift.

SERVING OTHERS

*There are different kinds
of service, but the same Lord.*
1 CORINTHIANS 12:5

God's gift of service has many forms. There are those who serve by being sensitive to the needs of others, those who expound on God's Word, those who cover others with prayer. Some serve by providing finances, others by giving their time in service to others. It pleases God when we serve each other, using the gifts He's placed in each of us. What a wonderful God to endow us with such generous and unique gifts.

Simplicity

A SIMPLE MESSAGE

The unfolding of your words gives light;
it gives understanding to the simple.
PSALM 119:130

. . . .

Jesus criticized the religious leaders of His day, saying that they had intentionally complicated faith in order to control the people. In fact, the message of faith is quite simple: God created us with the will to choose, and we chose to walk away. But through the sacrifice of His Son, Jesus, He bridged the gap between us—giving us a second opportunity to choose God. Some will accept His gift, and others will not. Nevertheless, He remains the God of second chances!

YES OR NO

*"All you need to say is simply 'Yes' or 'No';
anything beyond this comes from the evil one."*
MATTHEW 5:37

Children speak with such simplicity. Only as we grow older do we begin to fashion our words to make a point, influence others, and cover our mistakes. What different lives we would have if we refused to speak anything but the simple truth. The truth, delivered in love, is always best. It frees both the speaker and the hearer, making all communication transparent—without intention to deceive or mislead. It's a refreshing way to live!

Solitude

MOMENTS OF SOLITUDE

*[Your beauty] should be that of your inner self,
the unfading beauty of a gentle and quiet spirit,
which is of great worth in God's sight.*

1 PETER 3:4

. . . .

Our busy lives leave little room for solitude, but this is nothing new. The mother of John and Charles Wesley was said to have thrown her apron over her head in order to commandeer a moment of alone time. In other words, she did what she had to do to gain what she needed. We would be wise to follow her example. Our nerves need time to calm. . .our hearts need time to moderate. These little moments have the potential to make all of the other moments of life so much better.

ALONE TIME

It is good to wait quietly
for the salvation of the LORD.
LAMENTATIONS 3:26

• •

Many people never learn to appreciate solitude. When they sense a quiet moment, they do their best to fill it with whatever is closest—the television, radio, phone. . . They feel uncomfortable with their own thoughts. But God desires for us to feel at home with ourselves, to be certain of the words we speak and the things we do. He wants us to have confidence in what we believe and why, without needing the constant reinforcement of others. Give thanks to the heavenly Father today for moments of solitude when we need them most!

Strength

HE IS THE ONE

*The Lord God is my strength and
my might; he has become my salvation.*
ISAIAH 12:2 NRSV

. . . .

As women, we know what it's like to be strong for others when things go wrong. But who do we go to when we feel like we can't deal with one more bump in the road? God promises that He will be our strength when we are weak. He is an immovable mountain. . .the One who will hold on to us tightly and never let go. God is the One we can bare our souls to, and the only One with strength enough to keep us from falling.

TOUGH INSIDE

Those who hope in the Lord
will renew their strength.

ISAIAH 40:31

· ·

Physical strength is nice, but it's inner strength that really matters—that toughness that seeps up from our core and keeps us steady on our feet. That's the kind of toughness it takes to be a God follower. Without that rock-hard inner conviction, we would be tossed about, our faith challenged on every side. Thank God for the fortitude that comes when we truly know that He is on our side and always watching over us.

Spiritual Growth

ALL TERRAIN

*Neither the one who plants nor
the one who waters is anything,
but only God who gives the growth.*
1 CORINTHIANS 3:7 NRSV

. . . .

Spiritual growth, like physical growth, comes in spurts and starts. We may experience a time of intense revelation followed by a stretch so uneventful that it falls from our consciousness. This is the normal Christian life. The important thing is to keep things in perspective. When we feel full of understanding, we should remember that we have not yet arrived. When we feel bland and without direction, God has not abandoned us. Be thankful for both the slopes and also for the straightaways.

GOD'S HELPERS

*Grow in the grace and knowledge
of our Lord and Savior Jesus Christ.*
2 PETER 3:18 NCV

Growing in faith is like growing in any other way. It takes time and patience and the help of more mature God-followers in our lives. We may not recognize or even like these people at first. They won't be the ones who coddle us and tell us what we want to hear. They will be the ones who challenge us, call us out on our mistakes, and are there to hold us when we are filled with sorrow. Be thankful for these people who lead by Christ's example!

Surrender

FULL SURRENDER

There's an opportune time to do things,
a right time for everything on the earth. . .
A right time to hold on and another to let go.
ECCLESIASTES 3:1, 6 MSG

. . . .

There is, within each of us, a rigid, stubborn, inner person we call an ego. Our egos are only interested in personal gratification. And unless they are disciplined, we typically become narcissistic, vain, and selfish. When parents rightly discipline a child, those negative tendencies are brought under control—and kinder, gentler urgings begin to dominate. The same is true when we surrender our ways to God's control. And only then will our finest characteristics emerge.

TRUE GIFTS

*Commit your way to the LORD, trust also
in Him, and He shall bring it to pass.*
PSALM 37:5 NKJV

. . . .

Anyone who has watched a reality show that
specializes in singing has seen those poor, deluded
souls who claim that being a singer is their life's
dream; it's all that matters to them. Then they open
their mouths, and what comes out is horrifying. We
don't always know what's best for us—but God does.
He created us. When we surrender our wants and
desires for His, we come into alignment with our
true gifts and callings. We become winners.

Talent

FINDING YOUR GIFT

I have filled him with the Spirit of God,
with wisdom, with understanding,
with knowledge and with all kinds of skills.
EXODUS 31:3

. . . .

Some people have it all—beauty, grace, intelligence, and talent—while others wonder if they can do anything right. God has given a measure of talent to every person. Some just identify it sooner than others. The friend who has that amazing voice probably had no trouble identifying her talent. But for the rest of us, it may take some time trying our hands at new things. Ask God to help you find your giftedness, and then pursue it with a thankful heart.

TALENT MULTIPLIED

*Each of you should use whatever gift
you have received to serve others,
as faithful stewards of God's grace
in its various forms.*

1 PETER 4:10

. . . .

When it comes to talent, it's not how much we have, but rather how we use it that matters. God is pleased when we use our gifts to glorify Him and to bless others. In fact, talent is multiplied when it is freely given with thankful hearts to the enjoyment of those around us. We should never waste time thinking about what we can't do. Instead, we should focus our passions on what we can do.

Temptation

STAY AWAY

No temptation has overtaken you
except what is common to mankind.
And God is faithful; he will not let you
be tempted beyond that you can bear.
1 CORINTHIANS 10:13

Stay away from the pond, and you won't fall in. That's what a wise mother once said. And she's right. More often than not, we find ourselves falling to temptation because we place ourselves directly in temptation's path. It's wise to stay away from people and places where temptation can get a foothold. No matter how strong we think we are, it's always easier to walk around than to crawl out.

FLEE TEMPTATION

Submit yourselves, then, to God.
Resist the devil, and he will flee from you.
JAMES 4:7

. . . .

Even when we live wisely, there are times when temptation seems to be lurking around every corner. It might come through a media blast or arise out of an unexpected situation. We can't lock ourselves away from the world and refuse to deal with life. In times when we come face-to-face with temptation, God has given us a formula. First we are to ask for His help, then resist, and then quickly flee. Fleeing from temptation is not an act of cowardice; it's an act of obedience.

Testimony

BEING HONEST

Always be ready to make your defense to anyone
who demands from you an accounting
for the hope that is in you.
1 PETER 3:15 NRSV

Most of us are a little intimidated by the idea of talking to our friends about God. Will they think we're fanatics? Will they resent us or think we're being pushy? It shouldn't be that way. Every day we promote the things we like—a good book or a favorite movie. All God expects of us is to tell others what it's like to be His child when we're asked. And that's not being pushy—it's just being honest.

ACROSS THE TABLE

*"Let your light shine before others,
so that they may see your good works
and give glory to your Father in heaven."*
MATTHEW 5:16 NRSV

. . . .

It must be difficult to testify in court. Being questioned in front of all those people. . .all eyes on you. But sometimes that's what it takes to get to the truth. It's much easier when you find yourself across the kitchen table from someone who asks you to share what you know about God. You don't have to be a theologian. . . just a person who has discovered something amazing and wants to pass the good news along.

Time

ETERNITY

*[God] has also set eternity in the human heart;
yet no one can fathom what God has
done from beginning to end.*

ECCLESIASTES 3:11

. . . .

Even though we're ruled by clocks, most of us pay
minimal attention to the passing time. We live day
to day, trying to stay just one step ahead of life. One
day time will no longer matter. In fact, time will not
even exist. We won't grow older, aged by sorrows
and stress. Instead, we will be rightly aligned to
our Father's heartbeat for all of eternity, and that
is the only *tick- tock* we will be aware of. What a
wonderful day that will be!

IN OUR HANDS

A wise man's heart discerns
both time and judgment.
ECCLESIASTES 8:5 NKJV

• •

We live in a society driven by nonstop activity, rushing from one scheduled event to the next. Often so hurried we rarely have time to stop and think, reminisce, appreciate, be thankful. . . There will always be too many things on our to-do lists. But with God's help, we can sort through them and put an end to the rush and hurry. Then we can put activity in its rightful place. With the wisdom and guidance of the heavenly Father, we can have the power to take back our time and spend it as we see fit.

Trust

LEARNING TO TRUST

Trust in the LORD forever, for the LORD,
the LORD himself, is the Rock eternal.

ISAIAH 26:4

. . . .

We are born fully trusting creatures; and completely helpless, we depend on the goodness and care of others for our survival. But as we grow older, it becomes more difficult to trust. People fail us; they often let us down. Sometimes it may even seem wiser to take care of ourselves and trust no one. But there is someone we can trust unequivocally—and that is our never-failing God. And through trusting Him, we can learn to trust others again too.

HE SEES ALL

One who trusts in the LORD is secure.
PROVERBS 29:25 NRSV

. . . .

One thing is for sure: we don't know a single thing about what life has in store for us. We may know who we are and what has happened in the past, but we have no clue about the future. In fact, we can't see past this very moment—right here and now. But God asks us to trust Him, because He doesn't want us to move forward blindly. With His help—He sees all—we can walk down life's path with confidence.

Truth

DON'T BE FOOLED

*Buy the truth and do not sell it—wisdom,
instruction and insight as well.*
PROVERBS 23:23

. . . .

Anyone who has been involved in a bad car accident, injured in a terrible fall, or experienced a near drowning believes that truth is truth, no relativity there. Truth is absolute in the physical world and in the spiritual world as well. Something cannot be true just because we wish it were so. It either is or it isn't true! Don't be fooled by faulty philosophies. Truth doesn't change—period!

KNOWING THE TRUTH

*O LORD; Let Your lovingkindness and
Your truth continually preserve me.*
PSALM 40:11 NKJV

. . . .

Common sense would tell us that it's always better
to know the truth than to be aligned with lies. No
one wants to be a fool. But how do we know what
is true and what isn't in this smoke-and-mirrors
world in which we live? There is only one way:
God—who is truth—has promised to give us discernment. Sometimes the truth will be difficult to take
in and hard to accept, but it will always bring us
through.

Understanding

FREE TO UNDERSTAND

Who is wise and understanding among you?
Let them show it by their good life, by deeds
done in the humility that comes from wisdom.

JAMES 3:13

· ·

God has given us a great gift—the ability to understand. Of course, that gift only goes so far. Until we are with our Lord and our minds greatly unfurled, we cannot possibly comprehend everything. But we do have a measure of understanding and the free will to choose what we do with that knowledge. What God desires is for us to understand who He is and then freely choose to be in fellowship with Him.

UNCONDITIONAL LOVE

I gain understanding from your precepts.
PSALM 119:104

• •

With understanding comes responsibility and with responsibility comes accountability. These are big words but simple to comprehend. Because we have understanding, we are expected to behave responsibly and make good choices. But why would our choices be important to almighty God? Like a good parent, He loves us unconditionally and hates to see us suffer, especially when it's unnecessary suffering. Let's thank Him for the gift of understanding, and then work to be worthy of His gift.

LOOKING FOR MORE ENCOURAGEMENT FOR YOUR HEART?

Worry Less, Pray More

This purposeful devotional guide features 180 readings and prayers designed to help alleviate your worries as you learn to live in the peace of the Almighty God, who offers calm for your anxiety-filled soul.

Paperback / 978-1-68322-861-5 / $4.99

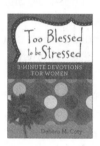

Too Blessed to be Stressed: 3-Minute Devotions for Women

You'll find the spiritual pick-me-up you need in *Too Blessed to Be Stressed: 3-Minute Devotions for Women.* 180 uplifting readings from bestselling author Debora M. Coty pack a powerful dose of inspiration, encouragement, humor, and faith into just-right-sized readings for your busy schedule.

Paperback / 978-1-63409-569-3 / $4.99